The Sun and the Sea

An African folktale

Retold by Elsie Nelley
Illustrations by Gregory Baldwin

Once upon a time,
Sun did not live in the sky.
He lived in a house near a beach.

Sun and Sea were friends.
Every day, Sun went down to the water
to talk with his friend.

One day, Sun said to Sea,
“I always come to see you.
You have never been to my house.”

“I would love to come,” said Sea.
“But I would have to bring my family, too.
Your house is too small for all of us.”

“No!” cried Sun. “My house is not too small. My house is big. Please come.”

“Very well,” said Sea.
“My family and I will come tomorrow.”

The next morning, Sun heard Sea call out, "Hello, my friend. My family and I are here."

Sun opened his front door.
Sea and some of her family
began to come inside Sun's house.

First, some brown crabs
crawled across the doorway.
Then, some small sea stars came in.

Sun smiled. “Your family is beautiful,” he said.

Soon, there was water all over the floor of Sun's house.

Lots of little fish were having fun chasing one another round and round.

But the water was getting higher and higher.
Sun stood on a chair.
Then, he climbed onto the table.

"Do you want me to take my family back home?" Sea asked Sun.

"No! Please, don't go," cried Sun.
"I think there will be room for everyone."

Sea looked around.
She knew that Sun's house
was going to be too small
for all of her family to fit inside.

Sun was surprised
when he saw some very big fish
splashing around under the table.

Then, Sun saw some sharks
waiting outside his front door.

“Do these sharks belong to your family, too?” he asked his friend.

But Sea did not hear him, because there was too much noise.

Now the water was nearly over Sun's head, so he quickly climbed onto the roof. But it was not even safe there, because the water kept creeping higher and higher.

Sun was scared. He didn't want to drown. So he jumped high above the clouds and into the sky.

Today, Sun stays up in the sky.

Now he only meets his friend, Sea,
early in the morning at sunrise,
and again at the end of the day at sunset.